Jane McDonald

The Untold Story of an English Singer and Television Presenter

Joe Copeland

2 | Jane McDonald: The Untold Story of an English Singer and Television Presenter

Copyright © 2024 [Joe Copeland]

All rights reserved. This work is protected by copyright law and may not be reproduced, distributed, transmitted, displayed, published, or broadcast without the prior written permission of the copyright owner. You may not alter or remove any trademark, copyright, or other notice from copies of the content. Unauthorized use and/or duplication of this material without express and written permission from the copyright owner is strictly prohibited. Excerpts and links may be used, provided that full and clear credit is given to [Joe Copeland] with appropriate and specific direction to the original content.

TABLE OF CONTENTS

INTRODUCTION 8

CHAPTER ONE 15

    Early Life and Roots 15

    The McDonald Family and Their Influence 16

    Discovering a Love for Music 18

    The Wakefield Connection 20

CHAPTER TWO 22

    The Path to Stardom 22

    From Weddings to Cruise Ships: Building a Career 23

    The Turning Point: The Cruise Documentary 24

    Chart-Topping Success 25

    Life after the Cruise 26

    Legacy of the Cruise 27

CHAPTER THREE 29

    Rising Fame and Musical Achievements 29

Chart-Topping Success: The Debut Album 29

Performing at Iconic Venues 30

Musical Versatility: Pop, Ballads, and Musicals 31

Memorable Live Performances 32

A Commercial Turnaround and Continued Success 34

CHAPTER FOUR 36

Breaking into Television 36

Joining Loose Women: A New Platform 36

The Birth of Cruising with Jane McDonald 38

Exploring the World: Holidaying with Jane McDonald 39

Winning a BAFTA: A Career Milestone 40

A Recording Contract with UMTV and BBC Guest Presenting 40

Leaving Loose Women After a Decade 41

CHAPTER FIVE 44

Life Beyond the Spotlight 44

Love and Loss: The Story of Eddie Rothe 45

Advocating for Charitable Causes 47

A Return to Her Roots 47

Living for the Moment 48

CONCLUSION 49

7 | Jane McDonald: The Untold Story of an English Singer and Television Presenter

INTRODUCTION

Jane McDonald stands as a shining example of what can be achieved with resilience, authenticity, and undeniable talent. Her story is one of grit, determination, and a passion for connecting with people through music and storytelling. Born on April 4, 1963, in the industrial town of Wakefield, West Yorkshire, Jane was the youngest of three children in a close-knit working-class family. Her father, Peter McDonald, was a miner, a profession synonymous with the hard-working communities of the region. Her mother, Jean, was a homemaker who served as the family's glue, instilling values of perseverance and kindness in her children.

Growing up, Jane's love for music was apparent from an early age. She was often found singing around the house or performing impromptu concerts for her family. Her parents encouraged her passion, even when the idea of pursuing a career in entertainment seemed like a far-fetched dream for a young girl from Wakefield. Jane's siblings also played a significant role in her early life, providing her with a sense of grounding that would stay with her throughout her journey.

Jane's road to success was far from smooth. After leaving school, she took on a series of odd jobs to support herself while nurturing her musical ambitions. She worked in local pubs, clubs, and social venues across Yorkshire, where she gained valuable experience as a performer. These gigs were not glamorous—Jane often had to deal with rowdy crowds, late-night commutes, and minimal pay—but they taught her the art of captivating an audience. Her powerful voice, tinged with soul and emotion, quickly became her trademark.

During these formative years, Jane often reflected on the challenges of breaking into the music industry. The club circuit in Northern England was notoriously tough, especially for a young woman trying to carve out her niche. Yet Jane persevered, driven by a belief in her talent and a determination to make her parents proud. These early performances were instrumental in shaping her career, teaching her not only the technicalities of live music but also the resilience needed to thrive in the industry.

In the 1980s, Jane took a significant step forward when she began working as a singer on cruise ships. This move marked a turning point in her life and career. Performing at sea allowed Jane to escape the constraints of her small-town upbringing and explore the world. It also introduced her to an entirely new audience—one that was as diverse as the passengers on board.

The cruise ship gigs were both demanding and rewarding. Jane was required to perform nightly, often adapting her repertoire to suit the tastes of international audiences. From classic ballads to upbeat show tunes, she mastered a wide range of genres, earning accolades from passengers and crew alike. It was during this period that Jane honed her ability to connect with people from all walks of life, a skill that would later become a cornerstone of her career.

Jane's big break came in 1998 when she became the star of the BBC docusoap The Cruise. The show followed the lives of crew members aboard the luxury cruise ship Galaxy, giving viewers a behind-the-scenes look at life on the high seas. Jane's natural charisma and breathtaking voice made her an instant standout. Whether she was belting out a power ballad or chatting candidly with the camera, she exuded a warmth and authenticity that resonated with audiences.

The success of The Cruise was unprecedented. Millions of viewers tuned in each week, and Jane quickly became a household name. Her newfound fame came with its challenges—adjusting to life in the spotlight was not easy—but it also opened doors she had only dreamed of. Shortly after the show aired, Jane released her self-titled debut album, which soared to the top of the UK Albums Chart and remained there for three weeks. This remarkable achievement solidified her status as one of Britain's most beloved performers.

Jane's music career blossomed in the years following The Cruise. She released several albums, many of which achieved commercial success and critical acclaim. Her musical style, a blend of pop, ballads, and musical theatre, showcased her versatility as an artist. From original compositions to heartfelt covers, Jane's songs often carried themes of love, hope, and resilience—reflecting her own journey.

Her live performances became legendary. Whether she was headlining at prestigious venues like the Royal Albert Hall or performing intimate gigs for her most loyal fans, Jane had an uncanny ability to make every audience member feel seen and appreciated. Her concerts were more than just musical events; they were celebrations of connection, joy, and shared humanity.

In addition to her success as a singer, Jane found a second home on television. In 2004, she joined the panel of ITV's daytime talk show Loose Women, where her quick wit and down-to-earth demeanor endeared her to viewers. She later ventured into travel programming with shows like Cruising with Jane McDonald and Holidaying with Jane McDonald, which combined her love of travel with her natural storytelling abilities. These programs not only showcased stunning destinations but also highlighted Jane's relatability and charm, earning her a BAFTA award in 2018.

Despite her public persona, Jane has always remained deeply private about her personal life. Her marriage to Henrik Brixen, whom she met during her cruise ship days, ended in divorce in 2003—a period she has described as one of the most challenging in her life. Years later, she found happiness with Eddie Rothe, her teenage sweetheart and former drummer of The Searchers. Their reunion was a heartwarming chapter in Jane's life, marked by love, laughter, and mutual support. Tragically, Eddie passed away in 2021, a loss that deeply affected Jane but also underscored her resilience.

Today, Jane McDonald is more than just a singer or television presenter; she is a cultural icon. Her ability to reinvent herself while staying true to her roots has made her a role model for countless fans. Whether she is belting out a show-stopping number, sharing travel tips on television, or simply connecting with her audience through social media, Jane continues to inspire.

Her story is a reminder that success is not just about talent—it's about perseverance, authenticity, and the courage to embrace change. From the clubs of Wakefield to the grand stages of the world, Jane McDonald's journey is one of extraordinary achievement and unwavering hope.

CHAPTER ONE

Early Life and Roots

Jane Anne McDonald was born April 4, 1963, in Wakefield, West Yorkshire, England. Her childhood was spent in this distinctive Yorkshire town known for its vibrant working-class culture, historic charm, and caring, close-knit communities. Wakefield was more than just her birthplace; it served as a steadfast anchor throughout her life and career.

Jane grew up in Yorkshire during the 1960s and 1970s, when she discovered simplicity and a feeling of community. Wakefield's combination of fast-paced city life and tranquil countryside makes it an ideal place to foster creativity and resilience. Jane often remembers her childhood days spent playing in neighborhood parks, exploring Miller Dam, and helping her family around the house. She recalls the cobblestone alleyways, bustling market squares, and local customs that gave her a sense of place and belonging.

Jane's first visit to Bridlington is still one of her most vivid childhood memories. Jane was ecstatic as a toddler when she first saw water. "I screamed the place down with excitement," she once said, describing how her mother, Jean, had to tighten her reins to keep her from running wild with joy. That day, young Jane complemented the North Sea, which sparked an unexpected outpouring of admiration. Moments like these—pure, unadulterated joy—define Jane's youth and influence her optimistic attitude on life.

Wakefield was more than a geographical location for Jane; it was a caring community with stories around every corner. She attended local schools, made lifelong friends, and learnt the importance of hard work and dedication. Jane grew up in a working-class neighborhood and witnessed directly the struggles and accomplishments of everyday people, which became a constant theme in her songs and public performances.

The McDonald Family and Their Influence

Jane's upbringing was centered on the McDonald family and their influence. The McDonalds epitomized the classic

Yorkshire family: close-knit, supportive, and deeply devoted to their traditions. Jane's parents, Peter and Jean McDonald, were influential in establishing her personality and ideals. Her father, a miner by trade, was recognized for his work ethic and unflinching commitment to providing for his family. Jane's mother, Jean, a homemaker, became her confidante and long-time collaborator.

The McDonald's home was filled with laughter, love, and music. Jean had an extraordinary capacity to bring the family together while teaching Jane the value of humility and thankfulness. Jane constantly discusses how her mother's wisdom and unwavering support helped her overcome life's obstacles. Even as an adult, Jane wanted to stay connected to her roots, so she rented a cottage in Wakefield with Jean to symbolize their close friendship.

Peter McDonald was both a hardworking miner and a skilled entertainer. He provided for his family financially by working as a handyman and, on occasion, a chimney sweep. But what truly set him apart was his ability to play the piano. Peter instilled in Jane a passion of music. On weekends,

Peter played the piano at the McDonalds' house, and Jane and her siblings joined in to sing their favourite songs. These musical family gatherings paved the way for Jane's future career in entertainment.

Peter's piano playing was more than a hobby; it brought the family together and created experiences Jane would cherish for the rest of her life. Jane frequently attributes her father for igniting her early love in music and performance, saying that his enthusiasm inspired her to dream large, even in the face of difficulty.

Discovering a Love for Music

Jane's love of music was clear from an early age. Jane was inspired to sing and act because she grew up in a creative household. Her first performances were spontaneous family concerts in the living room, where she sang along to her father's piano music. Throughout her adolescence, Jane's parents encouraged her to pursue her musical ability seriously.

As a child, Jane began singing in local clubs and nightclubs throughout Yorkshire. Despite their small size, these settings provided her with excellent experience and opportunities for socializing. She rapidly gained recognition for her powerful voice and captivating stage presence, which would later characterize her career. Singing in these private settings taught Jane the value of storytelling via song, which she perfected over time.

Jane's club performances were more than just stepping stones; they demonstrated her roots and determination to be loyal to herself. Unlike many ambitious entertainers who pursued fame and money in major cities, Jane preferred to practice her skill at home, finding inspiration from the people and places she knew best. Her capacity to connect with everyday people through her songs became one of her distinctive features.

Jane's passion and work ethic were evident from an early age. Balancing her singing concerts with day jobs required patience and determination, which set her distinct. Her performances wowed audiences not only with her vocal skills, but also with the honesty and love she poured into each song.

The Wakefield Connection

Jane has always had a close relationship with Wakefield. Despite her national and international success, she chose to remain in her hometown, demonstrating her beliefs and commitment to the community that supported her growth. "Wakefield is where I was born, where I went to school, where I was raised, and where I still live," Jane once said, underscoring her undying affection for her hometown.

Jane's upbringing in Wakefield was difficult, but it gave her the strength and will she needed to achieve. She usually credits her grounded personality and ability to connect with others to the ideals she learnt growing up in Yorkshire. Wakefield's love for her family, the support of her community, and the beauty of the surrounding countryside all had an impact on the person who would become a national treasure.

Jane constantly brings up Wakefield locales and events that are important to her in conversations. From hikes around Miller Dam to visits to local markets and businesses, her love for her community is evident in all facets of her life.

She recalls Miller Dam as a really inviting environment, one she wished to live near as a child and eventually did. "When I was a youngster, I used to promise myself, 'One day, I'm going to live as close as possible to this,' and now I do," Jane had once shouted.

CHAPTER TWO

The Path to Stardom

Jane McDonald's story began in Wakefield, Yorkshire, where she acquired a passion for music and performance while living in poverty. Her early career started in northern England's working men's clubs and taverns, which were known for their large crowds and hard schedules. For more than a decade, Jane toured the region, performing to small crowds in less than glamorous venues.

These clubs gave Jane more than just a stage; they taught her patience, character, and the ability to relate with people from many backgrounds. It was here that she honed her ability to read a room, adapt her repertoire to the mood, and deliver captivating performances night after night.

Jane's early performances were renowned for her powerful voice and kind manner. However, recognition was tough to come by. The audience was frequently more interested in the bingo or their beverages than in the actual performance onstage. Jane describes how the drapes were drawn over her mid-song, just as the bingo game was about to begin. Despite the challenges, she stayed determined.

"I considered myself successful even then," Jane later revealed. "I was doing what I loved, making a living from my gift, and bringing joy to people, even if it was on a small scale."

From Weddings to Cruise Ships: Building a Career

Jane's job forced her to venture beyond the pubs and clubs. She began singing at weddings and other occasions, showcasing her versatility and dedication to her craft. Her talent and expertise grabbed the interest of many in the entertainment industry, which led to her first cruise ship performances.

Her transition to cruise ship entertainment marked a watershed moment in her career, but it was not without challenges. Jane worked on several ships, including the Century, and faced payment delays, technical problems with sound equipment, and bad working conditions.

Disappointed, she briefly returned to club singing, convinced that life at sea was not for her.

However, the opportunity to perform as a vocalist aboard the luxury cruise ship Galaxy aroused her interest. The position was well-known in the cruise entertainment sector, and Jane's qualifications and expertise made her a strong candidate. What she didn't realize was that this decision would catapult her to new heights of fame.

The Turning Point: The Cruise Documentary

Jane's life altered significantly in 1998, when the BBC chose to broadcast The Cruise, a 12-part observational documentary series. Chris Terrill directed the series, which followed the Galaxy crew on their maiden trip to the Caribbean. Jane, then 34, had an important role in the series.

The first episode, Let the Dream Begin, aired on January 13, 1998, and soon drew 10.39 million viewers—a 41% audience share. Jane's performances and charm resonated with the crowd. Her warmth, wit, and honesty shone through, and she became a household name very immediately.

The series focused on more than just cruise ship management, emphasizing Jane's vocal abilities. Clips of her singing showed a voice that was both powerful and expressive, capturing audiences. Her lively nature and ability to interact with the camera helped her become the show's breakthrough star.

Following the success of The Cruise, the BBC aired two additional specials centered on Jane. The first, Jane Ties the Knot, is about her marriage to Danish plumber Henrik Brixen, whom she met while working on the Century. The wedding, which took place in the Virgin Islands, added a romantic touch to her evolving image. The second special, Jane's Cruise to the Stars, aired on December 31, 1998, capping out what Jane called "the most remarkable year of my life."

Chart-Topping Success

Following the documentary, Jane signed with independent record label Focus Music International. Jane McDonald's self-titled first album, released in July 1998, peaked at number one on the UK Albums Chart and remained there for three weeks. Jane's global recognition and emotional connection with her fans contributed to the album's success.

In addition to her album, Jane released the Christmas single Cruise into Christmas, a collection of seasonal favorites that reached number ten on the UK Singles Chart. During this time, she progressed from cruise ship performer to popular recording artist.

Jane was amazed by the transformation as she pondered on the preceding year. "I began 1998 as a largely unknown girl from Wakefield who had sung in so many clubs without ever being noticed by any really important people and ended the year as a household name," she says me with great pleasure. "It was unbelievable."

Life after the Cruise

The Cruise's breakthrough and following musical achievements opened up possibilities that Jane could only have dreamt. Her debut album was followed by a succession of smash singles, sold-out shows, and a growing presence on television.

Despite her unexpected success, Jane remained composed, reflecting on her early club and bar experiences with humility and gratitude for her achievements. She continues to push the boundaries, looking for new opportunities in music and television.

Legacy of the Cruise

For Jane McDonald, The Cruise was more than just a documentary; it marked the beginning of a decades-long career. The series not only demonstrated her intelligence, but also helped her become one of Britain's most popular performers.

Jane's connection to her cruise ship background remains strong now. Cruising with Jane McDonald, her BAFTA-winning series, pays tribute to the industry that propelled her to fame in the first place. Jane's songs, television appearances, and live performances continue to inspire and enchant fans around the world.

Her journey from singing in small bars to becoming a chart-topping performer and television personality displays determination, talent, and the ability to seize opportunities. Jane McDonald's climb to prominence was anything from normal; it was truly remarkable.

CHAPTER THREE

Rising Fame and Musical Achievements

Chart-Topping Success: The Debut Album

Few people could have predicted Jane McDonald's meteoric ascent to fame in 1998, when she became a household name owing to the BBC documentary series The Cruise. Her selflessness and outstanding singing gained a significant number of fans, and the exposure led to the extraordinary success of her self-titled debut album. Focus Music International issued the CD, which featured a collection of well-known covers that proved her talent to give classic songs new life.

The album's tracklist included timeless tunes such as "One Moment in Time," "The Wind Beneath My Wings," and "(You Make Me Feel Like a) Natural Woman." McDonald's emotive delivery and polished vocals enhanced these well-known tunes, adding a fresh, personal touch that attracted in her rapidly growing fan following. The album debuted at number one on the UK Albums Chart, which was a remarkable achievement for a relatively unknown artist at the time. This made her the first British female vocalist to have a debut album reach number one on the UK chart since Barbra Streisand.

The album's popularity spread outside the United Kingdom, reaching number 44 in New Zealand. Tracks like "Downtown" and "Have I Told You Lately" showcased her range, as she easily transitioned between upbeat melodies and somber ballads. Her ability to precisely and efficiently interpret these songs solidified her place in the music industry. According to the Official Charts Company, her debut album has sold 338,741 copies to date, indicating its continued success.

Performing at Iconic Venues

As her singing career progressed, McDonald's shows got increasingly popular with fans. She has performed in some of the UK's most prestigious venues, including the Royal Albert Hall and the London Palladium. These performances allowed her to showcase her dynamic range and establish a deep connection with her audience.

McDonald sold out the Royal Albert Hall, showcasing her celebrity and devoted fanbase. The grandeur of the setting complemented her great voice, providing spectators with an unforgettable experience. The London Palladium, with its long history of showcasing excellent vocalists, was the ideal setting for McDonald, who wowed the audience with her charisma and singing ability.

McDonald's tours were more than just singing songs; they were immersive experiences during which she told stories, engaged with the audience, and made each performance unique. These venues provided a perfect atmosphere for her to deliver captivating performances that left a lasting impression.

Musical Versatility: Pop, Ballads, and Musicals

Jane McDonald's ability to switch between musical styles is one of her most essential qualities as a performer. McDonald's voice is consistently fascinating and honest, whether she's singing a deep ballad, a catchy pop tune, or a stunning classical piece.

Her ability to remix popular songs demonstrated her versatility the most. Her debut album's singles "How Do I Live" and "You Don't Have to Say You Love Me" demonstrated her ability to personalize and profoundly interpret chart-topping hits. Similarly, her performances of musical theater classics proved her theatrical prowess and extensive knowledge of song-driven storytelling.

McDonald's performance as Grizabella in the musical Cats in 2015 proved her versatility even further. Her performance of "Memory" drove the crowd to tears, gaining her critical acclaim and solidifying her reputation as a fantastic performer. Whether on stage or in the studio, McDonald's ability to bridge genres has defined her career.

Memorable Live Performances

Jane McDonald's live performances are a high point of her career, characterized by passion, emotion, and a personal connection with her audience. Her tours have consistently sold out, with audiences drawn to her engaging stage presence and genuine contact.

One of her most memorable live performances came during her anniversary tour, which marked 20 years after her debut on The Cruise. These performances were a celebration of her career, blending old favorites with new material. The tour was a big success, with every place fully booked. Fans praised her candor as she revealed her travel experiences and thoughts, resulting in a deeply personal atmosphere.

McDonald's adaptability to shifting settings enhances the appeal of her live performances. She acts with the same zeal and conviction on a large stage as she does on a smaller scale, such as her television show Jane McDonald and Friends. Her Channel 5 presentations frequently include well-known songs about the topics of her travels, resulting in a distinct blend of music and storytelling.

Her role in Channel 5's Cruising With Jane McDonald series aided her live performance. McDonald's concert, which featured songs about her travels, was a commercial and critical triumph. This collaboration not only brought her music to new audiences, but it also reenergized her career, allowing her to spend a fourth week in the Top 10 with the Cruising With... album.

A Commercial Turnaround and Continued Success

Jane McDonald's capacity to adapt and prosper in an ever-changing entertainment industry demonstrates her resilience and strategic collaborations. According to Music Week, Absolute collaborated closely with Channel 5 to secure the success of her Cruising with... album. The plan used her existing recognition and the success of her television series to promote her music through cross-promotion and targeted advertising.

Absolute co-founder Henry Semmence described the collaboration as "fantastic," stating that it marks the beginning of a good relationship with Channel 5. The strategy consisted of selecting songs from her series that were relevant to the countries she visited and promoting them to the show's large viewership. This tactic not only increased album sales, but it also helped McDonald's status as a prominent player in the UK entertainment industry.

"She's had a solid fanbase whenever we put music to market," Semmence told me. "But obviously the Cruising With... series, which is delivering extraordinary viewing figures for Channel 5, has really pushed her profile right back up to the same level as when she was doing The Cruise 20 years ago."

The Cruising With... album and its success show McDonald's ability to evolve with the times, embracing new platforms and partnerships to keep her music contemporary and accessible. This rebirth has solidified her status as a beloved singer and entertainer, demonstrating that her light continues to shine brightly.

CHAPTER FOUR

Breaking into Television

Jane McDonald's transition to television was not only a natural extension of her musical abilities, but also a reflection of her charisma, relatability, and honesty. Her television career took off after she starred in The Cruise, a BBC docuseries about her life and job as a cruise ship entertainment. The show, which premiered in 1998, was a huge success, propelling McDonald into the spotlight. Her singing voice and down-to-earth manner won millions of viewers, paving the way for her move to television presenting.

Joining Loose Women: A New Platform

In 2004, Jane McDonald appeared on ITV's Loose Women, a daytime panel show where a group of women debate topics ranging from current affairs to personal experiences. The show gave Jane a new way to connect with her followers, not only through her music, but also through her wit, generosity, and opinions. McDonald, who appeared on the show three times per week, rapidly became a fan favorite. Her life experience and open attitude brought new perspectives to the discourse.

During her six-year tenure on the show, McDonald established herself as both a television personality and a popular character. However, she announced her resignation in 2010, citing a desire to continue her musical career and travel throughout the world, particularly to Australia and New Zealand. Although the Australian tour did not take place, McDonald had a terrific tour of the United Kingdom in 2011. She returned to Loose Women briefly in 2012 before leaving permanently in January 2014 to focus on her music and live engagements.

Even after leaving the show, McDonald has made guest appearances, and her stint on Loose Women remains a career highlight. It demonstrated her flexibility as a singer and solidified her standing as a household name outside of the music industry.

The Birth of Cruising with Jane McDonald

After leaving Loose Women, McDonald looked for additional options that complemented her passions in music, travel, and storytelling. Cruising with Jane McDonald, a travel and lifestyle series that aired on Channel 5 in 2017, marked her return to television. The show followed McDonald as she traversed the world on various cruise ships, blending her natural beauty with magnificent scenery.

The series was an ideal fit for McDonald. Her ability to engage the audience, combined with her understanding of the cruise business, elevated the event's educational and entertaining value. McDonald's personal touch, from interacting with crew members to sharing real moments from her adventures, distinguishes the series from other travel shows. Viewers found her relatable, whether she was eating local cuisine, taking part in on-board activities, or admiring the gorgeous scenery.

Cruising with Jane McDonald was quite popular, attracting individuals of all ages. It not only demonstrated her presenting abilities, but also solidified her place in British entertainment. The show's popularity led to spin-offs such as Holidaying with Jane McDonald, which expanded the concept to include land-based vacations.

Exploring the World: Holidaying with Jane McDonald

Following the success of Cruising with Jane McDonald, Channel 5 introduced Holidaying with Jane McDonald. This series enabled Jane to leave the cruise ships and explore different ways of transportation and pleasure. McDonald attended a variety of events, from luxury resorts to cultural luminaries, all with her trademark wit and enthusiasm.

The show highlighted her versatility as a broadcaster. McDonald's ability to connect with viewers was clear, whether they were participating in exciting events or learning about local cultures. She instilled reality in each account, capturing both the grandeur and the difficulties of travel.

Holidaying with Jane McDonald, like its predecessor, appeals to a diverse audience of readers, particularly those seeking vacation inspiration. McDonald's appealing style transformed each excursion into a vivid, personal story rather than simply a travelogue.

Winning a BAFTA: A Career Milestone

Cruising with Jane McDonald received the BAFTA Award for Best Feature in 2018, signalling a watershed moment in her film career. This was Channel 5's first BAFTA prize, which was a notable accomplishment. The prize recognized the show's quality, McDonald's outstanding presenting abilities, and the team's ability to produce engaging content that attracted viewers in.

Accepting the award was a watershed moment for McDonald, who thanked both the creative team and her dedicated fan base. The accolade solidified her status as one of Britain's most popular television personalities. It also demonstrated her ability to smoothly switch between music and television, achieving success in both.

A Recording Contract with UMTV and BBC Guest Presenting

Following her first number-one hit on an independent label, Jane McDonald got a recording contract with UMTV,

Universal's catalog and compilations division. This cooperation helped her reach a larger audience and enhance her profile in the music industry. During this period, she also appeared as a guest presenter on the BBC's National Lottery, demonstrating her flexibility as both a performer and broadcaster.

Leaving Loose Women After a Decade

Leave Loose Women Jane McDonald announced her retirement from Loose Women in 2014, after 11 years with the show. She announced in a poignant letter on Twitter that she would be taking a break to focus on her music. She wrote:

"I've had a terrific ten years on Loose Women and loved every minute of it. I have a busy and exciting year ahead of me, including a new album and a national concert tour. So it's time for me to move on from Loose Women and pursue new chances. I'm looking forward to meeting everyone again on tour, and I appreciate your ongoing support, devotion, and best wishes."

Fans and coworkers have different views to McDonald's decision. Her resignation signaled the end of an era while also creating exciting new opportunities for her career.

McDonald will take over as host of the British Soap Awards in June 2023, succeeding Philip Schofield. This significant portion emphasized her continued attractiveness and skill in a variety of television roles. Hosting the Oscars gave her the opportunity to connect with a live audience while also cementing her reputation as a reliable and engaging presenter.

Jane McDonald's television début was marked by inventiveness, honesty, and a genuine connection with her audience. From her early performances on Loose Women to her BAFTA-winning travel show and beyond, she has continuously demonstrated her versatility and popularity as an entertainer. McDonald's television career has not only increased her fan base, but has also demonstrated her ability to act in a variety of genres, establishing her place as a true icon in British culture.

As she continues to tour and take on new challenges, Jane McDonald shows the value of hard effort, tenacity, and remaining true to yourself.

CHAPTER FIVE

Life Beyond the Spotlight

Jane McDonald's ascent to popularity was not without obstacles. She was born and reared in Wakefield, West Yorkshire, and spent the majority of her childhood with her close-knit family. Jane was very close to her mother, Jean, whom she described as her "best friend." They shared a cottage at Newmillerdam, Wakefield, and lived there for many years. Jane was continuously complimenting her mother for being her anchor and support system during her years of playing on cruise ships and growing in fame.

Jane stayed at her family home even after her presence on The Cruise boosted her career. While her siblings, Tony and Janet, went about their lives and married, Jane remained at home, juggling the demands of her expanding business with the comfort and security offered by her mother.

In an honest interview, Jane revealed that she lived with her mother until the age of 45. "I was out working all the time and was able to pay my bills, and my mother was at home looking after me," she told me as a child. For Jane, this unusual arrangement worked wonders, allowing her to concentrate on her hard job while preserving close family ties. Jane was devastated when Jean died in 2018, but she remained determined to emulate her mother's perseverance and kindness.

Love and Loss: The Story of Eddie Rothe

Jane's romantic journey with Eddie Rothe is filled with both joy and grief. Eddie, the drummer for the band The Searchers, came back into Jane's life in 2008. They met briefly as children in 1980, but their careers diverged until decades later, when they reconnected. Their newfound romance took off swiftly, with Eddie proposing on Christmas Eve 2008, marking the beginning of a highly serious relationship.

For nearly a decade, Jane and Eddie had a life full with laughter, mutual respect, and common ambitions. They constantly expressed their delight, with Jane describing Eddie as a rock and an endless source of inspiration. Eddie was diagnosed with lung cancer, so their time together was cruelly cut short. He died on March 26, 2021, leaving Jane distraught.

After Eddie died, Jane expressed thankfulness for their time together, saying, "If we've learned anything over the previous year, it's that life is too brief. This has taught me that life is meant to be lived, and I plan to live it even more fully. Despite her loss, Jane has persevered, focusing on her work and inspiring others via her good attitude and grace.

Jane had several significant relationships before her romance with Eddie, including a marriage to Henrik Brixen, a Danish ship's plumbing engineer. The pair got married in 1998, and the ceremony was videotaped for a special episode of The Cruise. Henrik eventually became her manager, but the pressure on their relationship was too much. They divorced in 2003, and Henrik attributed the split to his lack of knowledge about the music industry. Jane previously married a man named Paul, about whom little is known.

Advocating for Charitable Causes

Jane McDonald's life behind the spotlight is defined by her commitment to give back. She has actively sponsored a wide range of humanitarian projects, including those reflecting her principles and personal experiences. Her high profile has enabled her to advocate for organizations dedicated to cancer research, mental health awareness, and caregiver support, spurred in part by her own experiences with Eddie's sickness and the death of her mother.

Jane's humanitarian efforts have extended to her hometown of Wakefield, where she has helped a variety of organizations and community events. She has regularly expressed her pride in her Yorkshire heritage and her desire to give back to the community that nourished her talent and drove her to prominence.

A Return to Her Roots

Throughout her broadcasting career, Jane has stressed her Yorkshire roots. Jane McDonald's Yorkshire, a Channel 5 series, lauded her home county's beauty, charm, culture, and history. The series captivated viewers by portraying the events and rituals that shaped Jane's personality.

Jane has continued to share her passion for life with audiences through this and other shows, such as Holidaying with Jane McDonald, demonstrating that pleasure and purpose can be found despite personal sorrow and hardship.

Living for the Moment

Jane McDonald's story exemplifies the power of resilience, love, and real living. Whether dealing with the highs of her job or the pain of losing loved ones, she has stayed determined to live life fully. Her tale is about humanity and elegance, not fame and wealth, and it inspires others to follow in her footsteps.

CONCLUSION

Jane McDonald's path exemplifies the power of resilience, authenticity, and unshakable passion. Born from humble beginnings in Wakefield, West Yorkshire, her life story epitomizes the traditional "rise to fame" storyline, defined by both remarkable accomplishments and terrible personal difficulties. Jane's journey as an artist and public personality, from singing in local bars to appearing on worldwide stages and television screens, portrays a person who has accepted her destiny with grace and tenacity.

Jane's rise was far from an overnight sensation. Her early years playing on cruise liners honed her discipline, modesty, and determination. During these encounters, she established her unique style, which is an intense, forceful vocal delivery that strikes a deep chord with audiences. Her breakthrough moment came with the 1998 BBC documentary The Cruise, which introduced her to millions of people and cemented her status as a national treasure. Her debut album's remarkable success, topping the UK charts for three weeks, validated her musical abilities and laid the groundwork for a successful career.

Jane distinguishes herself by her ability to switch between roles easily. Beyond music, she has had a huge impact on British television, anchoring popular shows including Cruising with Jane McDonald and Holidaying with Jane McDonald. These presentations not only highlight her lovely on-screen personality, but also exhibit her adventurous attitude and connection with the audience. Winning a BAFTA for her trip series in 2018 demonstrated her adaptability and the timeless appeal of her storytelling.

Jane's personal life has been filled with tremendous highs and tragic lows. Her marriage to Henrik Brixen, whom she met while on The Cruise, provided her delight but eventually resulted in divorce. Later, she reestablished a romance with her childhood sweetheart, Eddie Rothe, which brought her immense joy until his death in 2021. Through these experiences, Jane has shown great resilience, choosing to put her pain into her art and work, inspiring numerous people.

Jane's enduring appeal stems from her relatability. She is frequently referred to as "one of us"—a grounded, warm, and honest person who maintains true to her roots. Fans applaud her for remaining true to herself, never losing the sincerity that made her so popular from the start. Her ability to reconcile an illustrious career with a commitment to giving back, including participation in humanitarian endeavors, cements her legacy as both an entertainer and a compassionate human being.

Despite decades in the spotlight, Jane McDonald continues to innovate and inspire. Her recent endeavors, such as the "With All My Love" tour and special ship experiences, demonstrate her dedication to providing unforgettable encounters for her audience. As she looks to the future, it's clear that Jane is still motivated by her love of music, travel, and connection—a combination that ensures her relevance and effect will last for years.

Jane McDonald is more than just a singer and TV personality; she represents tenacity, reinvention, and joy. Her narrative demonstrates that success is more than just talent; it is also about the confidence to embrace change, humility to connect with people, and resilience to face life's challenges. For those who have followed her path, Jane is more than a performer; she is an inspiration. As she continues to pave her career, she leaves a legacy that extends beyond music and television, touching hearts and raising spirits in ways that few others can.

53 | Jane McDonald: The Untold Story of an English Singer and Television Presenter

Printed in Dunstable, United Kingdom